BUILD IT!

BAKE IT!

STENCIL IT! DO IT!

E IT! IT!

I LOVE YOU

GL

Mary Engelbreit's
AUTUMN

Mary Engelbreit's
AUTUMN
CRAFT BOOK

Illustrated by Mary Engelbreit
Written by Charlotte Lyons
Photography by Barbara Elliott Martin

ANDREWS AND MCMEEL
A Universal Press Syndicate Company
Kansas City

is a registered trademark of
Mary Engelbreit Enterprises, Inc.

10 9 8 7 6 5 4 3

Library of Congress Cataloging-in-Publication Data

Engelbreit, Mary.
    [Autumn craft book]
    Mary Engelbreit's autumn craft book / illustrated by Mary Engelbreit ; written by Charlotte Lyons ; photography by Barbara Elliott Martin.
        p. cm.
    Includes index.
    ISBN 0-8362-2229-6 (hd)
    1. Holiday decorations. 2. Handicraft. 3. Holiday cookery. 4. Cookery. I. Lyons, Charlotte. II. Title.
    TT900.H6E54 1996
    745.594'1-dc20   96-11116
                                                  CIP

Design by Stephanie Raaf

CONTENTS

one.
BACK
TO SCHOOL

SCHOOL BOOKS

*Success at school begins at home
so start the year with these decorated projects
that say schoolwork is fun!*

Traditional black and white composition note-books are perfect backgrounds for cover designs using paper and stickers. Make subject labels out of stationery products or just plain old copy paper cut to size. Title each with a permanent marker and paste securely to the cover. Flowers cut from construction or origami paper combine with rickrack and stickers to make each one special. Glue these into place and then seal your work with a coat or two of Mod Podge® to protect them from the daily grind.

back to school

BOOK BAG

*Even your teenager will love this
snazzy backpack perked up with vintage trims.*

Vintage shops often have small lengths of trims that are just the right amount for something special. A backpack uses less than a foot of woven sunflower trim to decorate the edges. A strip of black felt, cut into points with a pinking shear, adds more decoration, along with blanket-stitching on the edges. A medallion made from stacked buttons adds just the right touch of style and sophistication.

JEAN JACKET

*Your child will always know
which jacket is hers once you add
these personal touches from home.*

This jean jacket features an adorable pot holder,
fashioned by someone long ago. A quilting
square, or another interesting fabric, would also
work. A little blanket-stitching around the edges of
the potholder does the trick with very little effort
and matches the stitching style on the piece. Extra
charm comes from a few simple felt stars, a heart,
and an arrow sewn on the back. On the front, a star
and heart are appliquéd onto the pockets for a little
more fun.

back to school

PERSONAL PENNANT

*Celebrate your child's unique personality
with a pennant designed just for him.*

Brightly colored felt, cut and layered to spell a
child's name, fills the pennant center. Working
on a dark background makes the colors appear
more brilliant. A robot made from bits and pieces of
matching felt uses simple rectangles to build the
figure. To customize this for your child, choose a
scene or figure that reflects his or her special
interests. After laying out the design, glue all the
pieces down with fabric glue or white glue in small
amounts. Teacher's putty works well for hanging it
on the wall.

two.
HALLOWEEN

LUMINARIA

*Inspired by a vintage decoration,
this luminaria box casts the bewitching glow
of the season.*

Use our design or make your own ghostly silhouette that you can transfer to a 25" x 10" strip of black posterboard. Divide the strip into four equal sides 6" wide with an extra 1" tab to close the box. Score the folds with an X-acto® knife, but do not cut through the board. Draw your design onto the back of the second panel. Cut away the negative space to reveal the design as a silhouette. Apply orange tissue to the back with a gluestick and use the gluestick to close the box along the tab. A votive candle placed inside gives a wonderfully spooky, flickering light, but for safety reasons, you may want to illuminate with a flashlight.

GARDEN WITCH

*Enhance your fall garden
with the spirit of autumn playfulness that is
more welcoming than frightening.*

Cut a plywood scrap into a diamond shape 20" x 10", squaring one tip for the chin. Add a hat brim from a piece of lath or a paint stir stick. Paint the pieces as shown. Use either a 2x2, or a closet pole that is about 48" long, for the arms. Drape a yard of black vinyl over the pole like a kimono and cut double thickness for a dress. Apply fabric glue to the sleeves and side seams. Cover four empty cans with polkadotted vinyl and then string them onto twine fastened to the hem of the dress. Cut out black vinyl boots and attach these. Two pigtails of raffia are glued to the back of the face, which is then nailed onto the arms. The sunflowers are laced through the dress, along with painted cutouts and a broom.

halloween

BATIK

*Turn an old sheet into
a luminous stained glass window!*

Choose an empty wooden picture frame to determine the size of your design. Cut a clean, white cotton sheet to fit the dimensions of the frame and then draw a design in the center with a broad-tipped permanent marker. Paint the design with a wash made of thinned acrylic paints. Allow each color to dry before adding the next. When dry, paint over the design with melted paraffin and let dry. Bunch the cooled waxed fabric and immerse into a Rit dye bath as directed on the package. Rinse and dry on newspaper. Cover the cloth with paper towels and run a warm iron over the surface to remove the wax. The dye will permeate the design for the batik effect. Use a staple gun to stretch and mount the batik inside the frame.

BAT HOUSE

*Make the most of wood scraps
with this unusual bat house design.*

B egin with a pine box open on the bottom and
fit it with a vertical partition inside to divide
it into two chambers. Cover the inside walls with
plastic screening for the bats to hang from.
Decorate the outside with a hat, hair, and warty nose
cut from pine scraps. The cut edges can be whittled
with a utility knife to add a folk-art look. The eyes
are painted nail heads and the mouth is a zigzag
scowl cut from pine. Mount the box from eaves or on
a tree 10 to 15 feet high.

TRICK-OR-TREAT TOPIARIES AND HAT

*Use the dime store and your wildest dreams
to fashion these sweet topiary trees
and a holiday hat.*

Paint and decorate little clay pots to hold small trees full of gumdrops and other goodies (shown on previous page). Crows have nests of black jelly beans, sunflowers turn into bats, and lollipops grow alongside daisies. A group of these at the door wait for your favorite trick-or-treaters, who will rush to be counted among the first to ring your doorbell. While you're at it, make yourself a silly costume hat with the same sackful of fun (right).

PARTY BAGS

Brown lunch sacks are cleverly disguised in costumes of their own.

Construction paper, pipe cleaners, googly eyes, and pompons work a whimsical magic on plain old lunch bags. The Frankenstein robot is spray-painted silver and has bottlecap eyes. Telephone wire dangles from his neck. Silly spider carries a tiny purse, and the bumble bee clutches a daisy stem. Filled with party treats for the holiday, these will be coveted by your little guests.

halloween

SNACKY MASK

Maybe a mask is all you'll need for a costume. This one looks good enough to eat!

Decorate a plastic plate and doily with cookies and milk—and hot-glue for a one-of-a-kind disguise. Cut out the eyes and a nose vent and add the goodies into place. Add an elastic strap to secure it across the back. If you wish, wear it as a festive hat rather than a mask. Be creative and think of the many variations that are possible for this fun idea.

MAKE A NEST of PLEASANT THOUGHTS.

JOHN RUSKIN

three.
HOMECOMING

TAILGATE PICNIC

The glorious colors of the season remind us that these outdoor days are precious indeed.

For many, autumn means homecoming games and outdoor events that welcome food served picnic-style. Pack up some of these delicious foods and make a day of it! Our menu includes Tortilla Relish with chips, grilled chicken sandwiches—with red pepper slices and spinach leaves—on french bread, Vegetarian Chili, and gooey lemon bars for dessert. Some of the recipes are included on the following pages.

homecoming

TORTILLA RELISH

3/4 cup frozen corn
3/4 cup sliced black olives
3/4 cup chopped red pepper
2 tablespoons diced onion
2 minced cloves of garlic
1 teaspoon oregano
2 tablespoons lemon juice
4 tablespoons olive oil
1/3 cup white vinegar
salt
2 chopped ripe avocados

Combine ingredients, except avocados, the day before serving and refrigerate overnight. Just before serving, add two chopped ripe avocados and transfer to a flat dish. Serve with tortilla chips.

homecoming

VEGETARIAN CHILI

Cut one eggplant into 1" chunks and place in a small, shallow pan. Toss with 2 tablespoons olive oil, cover with foil, and bake at 350 degrees for 30 minutes. Heat 3 tablespoons olive oil in a casserole. Add 2 chopped onions and 3 minced cloves of garlic. Cook for 5 minutes. Add 2 diced zucchini, 2 large red peppers—cored and diced—and, if you like, a jalapeño seeded and finely minced. Cook 5 minutes. Add 4 diced fresh plum tomatoes, one 28-ounce can chopped tomatoes, 1/2 cup dry red wine, 2 tablespoons chili powder, 1 tablespoon dried oregano, 1 tablespoon ground cumin, 1 teaspoon fennel seeds. Add cooked eggplant; simmer 20 minutes. Add 1 cup canned white beans, the grated zest and juice of 1 large lemon, 1/3 cup chopped fresh cilantro or parsley, and ground pepper to taste. Simmer 5 minutes. Garnish with grated cheese and sour cream. Serves 8-10.

LETTER PILLOW

*Another way to enjoy
hard-earned letters of athletic achievement
is to put them on a pillow.
Even in a college dorm,
this is a cozy reminder of the past.*

Make a pillow from navy felt or polar fleece large enough to effectively frame the letters, trimming the edge with a border design in a matching school color. All that's left to do is blindstitch the school letters into place in the center. A sprinkling of shirt buttons adds extra appeal.

PENNANT RUG

A collection of souvenir pennants takes a turn beside a boy's bed as a novelty floor rug.

Arrange the pennants in a demilune shape with all the points touching in the center. Cut a felt backing larger than the arrangement and carefully pin and stitch the edges into place. As a decorative piece, it should be placed away from walkways that receive heavy traffic. This would also work exceptionally well as a headboard over a bed.

four.
LEAF
PEEPERS

CANDLE JARS

As summer slips away,
time spent outdoors is full of new sensations.
Twilight is quickly replaced with candlelight
as we linger in chilly air.
Make these candle jars wrapped with fall
decorations to replace the seashells of summer.

G lass canning jars are filled with sand halfway. Into this, sink a white candle to the bottom. Wrap the top edge with a length of raffia and tie leaves, berries, and harvest corn ornaments onto the outside. Be sure the decorations do not hang too close to the opening where the flame will flicker. Set among colorful autumn gourds, these candle jars create a lovely still life in the dusk.

leaf peepers

APPLE BREAD

Autumn means crisp apples
and cooler days for baking.
If you are lucky enough to fill a day
and your pantry with the delight
of picking your own, you will welcome
another good recipe to use up the excess.

B eat 3/4 cup vegetable oil with 1 cup white or brown sugar and 2 eggs. Stir in 1-1/2 cup chopped, unpeeled apples, 1/4 cup chopped walnuts, and 1 tablespoon grated lemon zest, if you like. Sift together 1-1/2 cup flour, 1 teaspoon cinnamon, 1/2 teaspoon nutmeg, 1 teaspoon baking soda, and 1/4 teaspoon salt. Add to apple mixture. Do not overmix. Pour into a 9" x 5" loaf pan. Bake at 350 degrees for 55 to 60 minutes.

CANNING LABELS

*Jams and jellies from the kitchen are
sweet reminders of the pleasures of summer.
Make special labels that distinguish yours
with an extra homemade touch.*

A few permanent markers and simple scenes
of farmhouses and trees transform squares
of brown craft paper cut right from a lunch sack.
A little scalloped border encloses the label with
a decorative framework. Glue these onto filled
canning jars with rubber cement and decorate
the tops with colorful tissue paper caps secured
with a ribbon tie. A button glued or sewn to the
bow is a great finish.

leaf peepers

COOKIES FOR BIRDS

*Your children will love this thoughtful and
creative offering.
Be sure to hang them close enough to a window
so that everyone can watch
the birds' appreciative nibbling.*

Make sugar cookies with vegetable shortening
instead of butter. Refrigerate the dough for
an hour, then roll out and cut into free-form bird
shapes. If you like, make a paper pattern first to use
as a guide. Bake as your recipe suggests and use a
bamboo skewer to poke a hole into the top as soon as
they come out of the oven. Cool and frost with
peanut butter. Press bird seed and harvest corn ker-
nels into cookies to decorate. Hang from trees with
twine or ribbon.

FALL FLEA MARKET

*An outdoor antique market on a fall weekend
is a favorite way to gather finds
and inspiration for project ideas.*

Any glorious day will do, but go as early as possible. Bundle up and head for the hills where cheap thrills await your discovery. Walking shoes, a keen eye, and sharp bargaining skills help ferret out the best market treasures. Inspiration or your heart's desire comes unexpectedly at a flea market, so be prepared to make quick, confident decisions. Don't pass up something you have a strong feeling about—chances are it won't be there when you go back.

leaf peepers

TWIG LAMP SHADE

Dress up a plain lamp shade with cuttings from the garden and potato prints.

Purchase a lamp shade from the department store that fits a lamp you have. Use a potato and an X-acto® knife to carve a leaf stem stamp. Apply gold acrylic paint with a brush to the stamp and press your design randomly all over the shade. Practice on newspaper and then begin at the shade seam so that you develop your best technique by the time you are working on the front. Allow to dry. Cut several straight canes from a backyard shrub (like mock orange) and remove the leaves. Carefully cut the sticks into custom lengths and glue these with hot-glue (or white glue which dries clear) to the shade from top edge to bottom, filling the horizontal spaces with smaller pieces as you go. Allow to dry undisturbed overnight.

leaf peepers

FANCY VEST

*A thrift shop suit vest
becomes a whimsical collage of cutouts
and costume jewelry accents.*

Make wool felt by washing wool fabric in hot water and then drying it in the dryer. Make character cutouts from this felt and blanket-stitch them onto the front panels of a second-hand vest. You can use cookie cutters for patterns if you wish. Trim pockets in strips of colorful wool and combine with lace snippets here and there. A few old star buttons sparkle above a little house, the ribbon on the pocket holds a little key and a bluebird pin soars with happiness over all. Experiment with felt images that are easy to build by stacking simple shapes in bright wool colors. It's easier than you think.

five.
THANKSGIVING

STENCILED APRON

*Thanksgiving calls for an abundance
of time spent in the kitchen.
Dress up the cook with a hand-stenciled apron
made especially to celebrate the occasion.*

Begin with a plain white canvas apron. Develop or purchase a main stencil design for the center of the bib. Make a secondary overall pattern stencil such as the cherry sprig shown here. Another cutout for the checkerboard should be cut to the measurements of the pocket or hem. Use a sponge and acrylic or fabric paints to apply the stencil colors. Practice on newspaper to achieve the desired effect before working on the apron. After taping into place and painting the main design, paint the checkerboard wherever you have planned to do so. Then scatter the cherries, with and without leaves, here and there. When dry, press with a hot iron to set the paints.

HARVEST TABLE

*For this holiday that celebrates
our heritage and harvest, set the table
with personal treasures
that evoke nostalgic thoughts.*

Every guest at the table revels in the table setting presented before him. Each place setting
here has the offering of an unusual object with a
history that inspires conversation or reverie. A
handful of filberts peppers a beautiful kilim used as
a table covering. Grandfather's pocket watch invites
inspection beside cut crystal glasses. Using the doc-
ument boxes to build pedestals and partitions for
each arrangement creates height and interest without obstruction. Although everyone is gathered to
share food and company, the delight inspired by
these lovely objects adds another pleasure to the
day.

DECOUPAGED CAKE PLATE

*Create an elegant serving piece
with paper cutouts and a glass dish.*

B egin with a clean glass cake plate. Use copyright-free engravings (such as those found in Dover publications) and copy them onto ivory copy paper. Copy an old letter to make two sheets of ivory background paper. Cut out the images and arrange them beneath the glass. Cut a ring of gold tissue paper to fit the outside edge of the dish. Mix vinyl wallpaper paste to a milky consistency. Use a foam brush and paint the surface of each cutout, applying it to the underneath side of the glass, face up. Smooth out all bubbles and wrinkles. Apply a backing cut from the letter with the same technique and paste. Paint the back of your finished work with two coats of Mod Podge®. Wipe surface to clean.

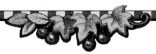

ELEGANT PURSES

*Splendid fabrics make luxurious daybags
for shopping and visiting.*

Richly textured velvets and brocades combine
with sumptuous satins and silks in these
lovely daybags. Use a store-bought pattern and
exquisite dressmaker trimmings to make these
loosely constructed purses. Contrasting lining fabrics and carefully chosen buttons for fine details
will make them favorites for all occasions.

thanksgiving

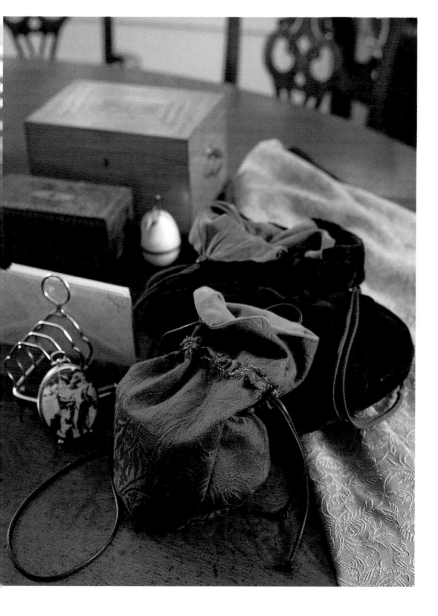

TURKEY POTPIE

Leftovers never looked or tasted so good
as they will in this savory potpie.

Sauté 1 cup chopped onions in 2 tablespoons oil for 3 minutes. Melt 2 tablespoons butter in a heavy saucepan. Add 3 tablespoons flour and cook for a couple of minutes. Add 3/4 cup chicken broth and cook slowly, whisking to thicken. Cool slightly. Add 3/4 cup half-and-half. Add 1 cup chopped carrots, 2 cups chopped turkey, 3 cups cooked rice, and broth-cream mixture to onion mixture in the skillet. Heat for 3 minutes. Season with 1 teaspoon curry powder, 1/2 teaspoon ground sage, and salt and pepper to taste. Pour into a deep-dish pie pan and top with piecrust. Cut slits in crust and decorate with turkey cutouts. Brush crust with a mixture of egg yolk beaten with 1 tablespoon cream. Bake at 375 degrees for 35 minutes. Serves 4.

thanksgiving

CONTRIBUTORS

Project Designs

Charlotte Lyons: School Books, Book Bag, Jean Jacket,
Personal Pennant, Luminaria, Garden Witch, Batik,
Letter Pillow, Pennant Rug, Canning Labels,
Twig Lamp Shade, Fancy Vest, Stenciled Apron,
Decoupaged Cake Plate

Nicki Dwyer: Tailgate Picnic, Apple Bread,
Cookies for Birds, Turkey Potpie

Jesse Hickman: Bat House

Alice Newquist: Witches and Goblins

Jeff O'Connor: Jack-o'-Lanterns

Project Designs-continued
Holly Saunders: Elegant Purses

Joseph Slattery: Trick-or-treat Topiaries and Hat,
Party Bags, Snacky Mask

Sally Weaver: Candle Jars

Grateful Appreciation to
Frank and Kathy Curotto
Jim Dwyer
Linda Solovic and Gary Karpinski
Rosalind Reed
Suzy and Sam Stout
Marie and Bill Trader
Robin Winge and Michael Dinges
Lakewood Antique Market, Atlanta, Georgia
Oak Park and River Forest High School
Jean Lowe, Stephanie Raaf, Stephanie Barken,
and **Dave Bari**

INDEX